This book
belongs to

52 WORDS

with the power and potential to transform your life

Art & Design by Karla Dornacher

karladornacher.com • karladornacher.etsy.com * facebook.com/karladornacher • instagram.com/karladornacher
Karla Dornacher Designs
Vancouver, WA 98664

52 WORdS

52 Words is a beautifully illustrated coloring book designed to inspire you to color creatively and live with more clarity...
whether you're choosing your One Word to focus on for the year or simply coloring a word a week to encourage you along the way.

Grounded in scripture, these 52 Words were chosen for their power and potential to draw you closer to God,
influence the decisions you make, and motivate you to live a full and joy-filled life.

Each single-sided page features an illustrated word for coloring and a scripture verse to meditate on and memorize...
followed by a single-sided journal page with prompts to record your thoughts and prayers.

And remember... there is no right or wrong way to color!
It's all about enjoying the process... choosing your own color palette... unleashing your own inner artist!
My designs are perfect for crayons, colored pencils, watercolor pencils, markers, and gel pens.

When using colored pencils you can add depth of color by layering darker tones over light ones.
To help prevent colors from bleeding through the back side of the page when using water or marker
place a blank sheet of paper between the pages when coloring.
For color pencil tips and techniques please visit my website www.karladornacher.com

The designs in this book are printed on the front of the pages only to enable you to remove them from the book
and trim to fit an 8"x8" frame... perfect for your own home or for gift giving!

May God bless the creativity of your heart and hands...
with His love and for His glory...
Karla

Contents

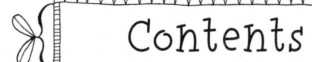

52 inspiring Words
to encourage your heart and lift your spirit!

Use this page to test your colored pencils, markers, or paints... or draw your own word or doodles to color!
And don't forget to place a sheet of paper or card stock between the pages to help guard against bleeding through.

♡ Hello my beautiful friends! ♡

We all know that words have power. There is a proverb in the Bible that tells us that life and death are in the power of the tongue... in other words.. the words we speak... to ourselves and to others... can build up and encourage or tear down and destroy. I am excited to share with you these 52 WORDS that have the power and potential to not only encourage your heart but to truly transform your life.

I believe there are three distinct ways
you can enjoy and benefit from this coloring book...

1, Color simply for the fun of it! You can randomly choose the words and designs that resonate with you the most and just enjoy some rest and relaxing time with God as you color.

2. Make it a 52 Week Journey by choosing to color one word to focus on for an entire week throughout the year. Taking this approach gives you the time to dig a little deeper. look up the definitions. Meditate on the accompanying Bible verses or choose your own. And ask God to use that word to speak wisdom and power into your life throughout the week before moving onto the next one. As you focus on the word of the week, think about what it means to you... how it might impact and influence your choices, your relationships, and your perspective of the world around you for good. And lastly, ask God to show you what you can do... what action you can take to live this word out in greater ways in your everyday life.

3. You might also want to use the words and verses in this coloring book to help you choose your own ONE WORD... your GOD WORD... to focus on for the entire year. As you turn the pages and ponder the potential of each word, ask God to begin to reveal the ONE WORD He wants for you. You might begin by choosing and coloring a few words that really resonate with you and, as you color, think about what each word means to you and how God might want to use it to draw you closer to Himself and how He might use it in order to continue the work that He has already begun in you... and through you... for His glory and praise!

However you choose to color your way through these 52 WORDS, I pray each one is a blessing to you!

Love and God-hugs...

Karla ♡

For I know the plans I have for you," declares the Lord, "plans to prosper you and not to harm you, plans to give you hope and a future.

Jeremiah 29:11

What does this word mean to you?

How might focusing on this one word transform your life?

Does this word reflect what you're longing to see God do in you & through you?

So then faith comes by hearing, and hearing by the word of God.

Romans 10:17

What does this word mean to you?

How might focusing on this one word transform your life?

Does this word reflect what you're longing to see God do in you & through you?

We must keep our eyes on Jesus, who leads us and makes our faith complete.

Hebrews 12:2 CEV

What does this WORD mean to you?

How might focusing on this one WORD transform your life?

Does this WORD Reflect what you're longing to see God do in you & through you?

A new commandment I give to you, that you love one another:
just as I have loved you, you also are to love one another.

John 13:34

What does this word mean to you?

How might focusing on this one word transform your life?

Does this word reflect what you're longing to see God do in you & through you?

Therefore, as God's chosen people, holy and dearly loved, clothe yourselves with compassion, kindness, humility, gentleness and patience.

Colossians 3:12

What does this word mean to you?

How might focusing on this one word transform your life?

Does this word reflect what you're longing to see God do in you & through you?

Delight yourself in the Lord and He will give you the desires of your heart.

Psalm 37:4

What does this word mean to you?

How might focusing on this one word transform your life?

Does this word reflect what you're longing to see God do in you & through you?

Let everything that has breath praise the Lord.

Psalm 150:6

What does this WORD mean to you?

How might focusing on this one word transform your Life?

Does this WORD Reflect what you're longing to see God do in you & through you?

Blessed is she who has believed that the Lord would fulfill his promises to her!

Luke 1:45

What does this word mean to you?

How might focusing on this one word transform your life?

Does this word reflect what you're longing to see God do in you & through you?

Rejoice always, pray without ceasing,
give thanks in all circumstances; for this is the will of God in Christ Jesus for you.
1 Thessalonians 5:16-18

What does this word mean to you?

How might focusing on this one word transform your life?

Does this word reflect what you're longing to see God do in you & through you?

The joy of the Lord is your strength.

Nehemiah 8:10

What does this WORD mean to you?

How might focusing on this one WORD transform your life?

Does this WORD Reflect what you're longing to see God do in you & through you?

For you, O Lord, have made me glad by your work; at the works of your hands I sing for joy.

Psalm 92:4 NIV

What does this word mean to you?

How might focusing on this one word transform your life?

Does this word reflect what you're longing to see God do in you & through you?

Then you will know the truth, and the truth will set you free.

John 8:32

What does this WORD mean to you?

How might focusing on this one WORD transform your life?

Does this WORD REFLECT what you're longing to see God do in you & through you?

If we confess our sins,

he is faithful and just and will forgive us our sins and purify us from all unrighteousness.

1 John 1:9

What does this word mean to you?

How might focusing on this one word transform your life?

Does this word reflect what you're longing to see God do in you & through you?

You are the light of the world... let your light shine before others,
That they may see your good deeds and glorify your Father in heaven.

Matthew 15:14, 16

What does this word mean to you?

How might focusing on this one word transform your life?

Does this word reflect what you're longing to see God do in you & through you?

Whoever sows sparingly will also reap sparingly, and whoever sows generously will also reap generously.

2 Corinthians 9:6

What does this WORD mean to you?

How might focusing on this one WORD transform YOUR life?

Does this WORD Reflect what YOU'RE longing to See God do in you & through you?

Being confident of this, that he who began a good work in you
will carry it on to completion until the day of Christ Jesus.

Philippians 1:6

What does this WORD mean to you?

How might focusing on this one WORD transform your life?

Does this WORD Reflect what you're Longing to See God do in you & through you?

Live a life worthy of the Lord and please him in every way: bearing fruit in every good work, growing in the knowledge of God,

Colossians 1:10

What does this WORD mean to you?

How might focusing on this one WORD transform your life?

Does this WORD Reflect what you're longing to see God do in you & through you?

But one thing I do: forgetting what lies behind and straining forward to what lies ahead,
I press on toward the goal for the prize of the upward call of God in Christ Jesus.

Philippians 3:13-14

What does this word mean to you?

How might focusing on this one word transform your life?

Does this word reflect what you're longing to see God do in you & through you?

And let the peace of Christ rule in your hearts, to which indeed you were called in one body.

Colossians 3:15

What does this word mean to you?

How might focusing on this one word transform your life?

Does this word reflect what you're longing to see God do in you & through you?

Look carefully then how you walk, not as unwise but as wise, making the best use of the time, because the days are evil. Therefore do not be foolish, but understand what the will of the Lord is.

Ephesians 5:15-17

What does this WORD mean to you?

How might focusing on this one WORD transform your Life?

Does this WORD REFLECT what you're longing to see God do in you & through you?

Whatever happens, conduct yourselves in a manner worthy of the gospel of Christ.

Philippians 1:27

What does this word mean to you?

How might focusing on this one word transform your life?

Does this word reflect what you're longing to see God do in you & through you?

Restore to me the joy of Your salvation, And uphold me by Your generous Spirit.

Psalm 51:12

What does this word mean to you?

How might focusing on this one word transform your life?

Does this word reflect what you're longing to see God do in you & through you?

Give thanks in all circumstances; for this is the will of God in Christ Jesus for you.

1 Thessalonians 5:18

What does this word mean to you?

How might focusing on this one word transform your life?

Does this word reflect what you're longing to see God do in you & through you?

For where your treasure is, so there your heart will be also.

Luke 12:34

What does this WORD mean to you?

How might focusing on this one WORD transform your Life?

Does this WORD Reflect what you'Re Longing to See God do in you & through you?

Rejoice in the Lord always: and again I say, Rejoice.

Philippians 4:4

What does this WORD mean to you?

How might focusing on this one word transform your life?

Does this WORD Reflect what you're longing to see God do in you & through you?

Those who are planted in the house of the Lord Shall flourish in the courts of our God.

Psalm 92:13

What does this WORD mean to you?

How might focusing on this one WORD transform YOUR Life?

Does this WORD Reflect what you'RE LonginG to See God do in you & through you?

Now to him who is able to do immeasurably more than all we ask or imagine,
according to his power that is at work within us.

Ephesians 3:20

What does this word mean to you?

How might focusing on this one word transform your life?

Does this word reflect what you're longing to see God do in you & through you?

Come to me, all you who are weary and burdened, and I will give you rest. Take my yoke upon you and learn from me, for I am gentle and humble in heart, and you will find rest for your souls. For my yoke is easy and my burden is light.

Matthew 11:28-30

What does this WORD mean to you?

How might focusing on this one WORD transform YOUR Life?

Does this WORD Reflect what you're Longing to See God do in you & through you?

Have I not commanded you? Be strong and courageous. Do not be afraid; do not be discouraged, for the Lord your God will be with you wherever you go.

Joshua 1:9

What does this word mean to you?

How might focusing on this one word transform your life?

Does this word reflect what you're longing to see God do in you & through you?

God created man in his own image, in the image of God he
created him; male and female he created them.

Genesis 1:27

What does this WORD mean to you?

How might focusing on this one WORD transform your life?

Does this WORD Reflect what you're longing to see God do in you & through you?

I am the vine, you are the branches.

He who abides in Me, and I in him, bears much fruit; for without Me you can do nothing.

John 15:5

What does this word mean to you?

How might focusing on this one word transform your life?

Does this word reflect what you're longing to see God do in you & through you?

And God is able to make all grace overflow to you so that,

because you have enough of everything in every way at all times, you will overflow in every good work.

2 Corinthians 9:8

What does this WORD mean to you?

How might focusing on this one WORD transform your Life?

Does this WORD Reflect what you're Longing to See God do in you & through you?

So if the Son sets you free, you will be free indeed.

John 8:36

What does this WORD mean to you?

How might focusing on this one WORD transform your life?

Does this WORD Reflect what you're longing to see God do in you & through you?

...present yourselves to God as those who have been brought from death to life, and your members to God as instruments for righteousness.

Romans 6:13

What does this WORD mean to you?

How might focusing on this one WORD transform your Life?

Does this WORD Reflect what you're longing to See God do in you & through you?

Call to Me, and I will answer you, and show you great and mighty things, which you do not know.

Jeremiah 33:3

What does this WORD mean to you?

How might focusing on this one WORD transform your life?

Does this WORD reflect what you're longing to see God do in you & through you?

I came that they may have and enjoy life, and have it in abundance

John 10:10

What does this WORD mean to you?

How might focusing on this one word transform your life?

Does this WORD Reflect what you're longing to See God do in you & through you?

And do not be conformed to this world, but be transformed by the renewing of your mind,

so that you may prove what the will of God is, that which is good and acceptable and perfect.

Romans 12:2

What does this word mean to you?

How might focusing on this one word transform your life?

Does this word reflect what you're longing to see God do in you & through you?

Not that I speak from want, for I have learned to be content in whatever circumstances I am.

Philippians 4:11-13

What does this WORD mean to you?

How might focusing on this one WORD transform your life?

Does this WORD Reflect what you're longing to see God do in you & through you?

The Lord is close to the brokenhearted and saves those who are crushed in spirit.

Psalm 34:18

What does this WORD mean to you?

How might focusing on this one word transform your life?

Does this WORD Reflect what you're longing to See God do in you & through you?

Ask, and it will be given to; seek and you will find; knock and the door will be opened to you.

Matthew 7:7

What does this word mean to you?

How might focusing on this one word transform your life?

Does this word reflect what you're longing to see God do in you & through you?

If any of you lacks wisdom, you should ask God, who gives generously to all without finding fault, and it will be given to you.

James 1:5

What does this word mean to you?

How might focusing on this one word transform your life?

Does this word reflect what you're longing to see God do in you & through you?

The Spirit of the Lord God is upon Me, because the Lord has anointed Me to preach good tidings to the poor;

He has sent Me to heal the brokenhearted, to proclaim liberty to the captives,

and the opening of the prison to those who are bound.

Isaiah 61:1

What does this WORD mean to you?

How might focusing on this one word transform your life?

Does this WORD Reflect what you're longing to see God do in you & through you?

Declare His glory among the nations, His wonders among all peoples.

Psalm 96:3

What does this WORD mean to you?

How might focusing on this one word transform your Life?

Does this WORD Reflect what you're Longing to See God do in you & through you?

But you are a chosen generation, a royal priesthood, a holy nation, His own special people, that you may proclaim the praises of Him who called you out of darkness into His marvelous light.

1 Peter 2:9

What does this word mean to you?

How might focusing on this one word transform your life?

Does this word reflect what you're longing to see God do in you & through you?

But by the grace of God I am what I am, and His grace toward me was not in vain; but I labored more abundantly than they all, yet not I, but the grace of God which was with me.

I Corinthians 15:10

What does this WORD mean to you?

How might focusing on this one WORD transform your life?

Does this WORD Reflect what you're Longing to see God do in you & through you?

In everything set them n example by doing what is good.

Titus 2:7

What does this WORD mean to you?

How might focusing on this one WORD transform your Life?

Does this WORD Reflect what you're Longing to See God do in you & through you?

And we all, with unveiled face, beholding the glory of the Lord,

are being transformed into the same image from one degree of glory to another.

2 Corinthians 3:18 ESV

What does this word mean to you?

How might focusing on this one word transform your life?

Does this word reflect what you're longing to see God do in you & through you?

Whatever things are lovely... think on these things.

Philippians 4:8

What does this WORD mean to you?

How might focusing on this one WORD transform your Life?

Does this WORD Reflect what you're Longing to See God do in you & through you?

A merry heart does good, like medicine.

Proverbs 17:22

What does this word mean to you?

How might focusing on this one word transform your life?

Does this word reflect what you're longing to see God do in you & through you?

For everyone who has been born of God overcomes the world.
And this is the victory that has overcome the world—our faith.

1 John 5:4

What does this WORD mean to you?

How might focusing on this one WORD transform your life?

Does this WORD Reflect what you're longing to see God do in you & through you?

By this my Father is glorified, that you bear much fruit and so prove to be my disciples.

John 15:8 ESV

What does this WORD mean to you?

How might focusing on this one word transform your life?

Does this WORD reflect what you're longing to see God do in you & through you?

For is it man's favor or God's that I aspire to?

Galatians 1:10

My dear friend...
Thank you again for buying this *52 Words* Coloring Book.
I hope you have delighted in some special moments with God,
and found a little rest for your soul in His Word along the way.
And I hope you've been inspired and encouraged to be creative and clever
in your own personal expression of color and play...
and maybe even discovered your ONE WORD for the new year!

For more inspiration, free downloads, and current news and updates visit:
www.karladornacher.com
www.facebook.com/karladornacher
www.instagram.com/karladornacher
www.youtube.com/c/karladornacher

To shop for more "Color Your Own" digital art including Bible bookmarks and
Blessing Cards... as well as my fine art prints... please visit:
www.karladornacher.etsy.com

God bless you and keep you...
in His love... and always for His glory...
Karla

Made in the USA
Coppell, TX
23 April 2021